# Peculiar Clothing

by
Lawrence L. Graham

# Peculiar Clothing

> *Because of the dynamic
> nature of the Internet, any
> addresses or web links
> contained in this book may
> have changed since
> publication and may no
> longer be valid.*

Cover Art and Illustrations
by the Author

Printed in the United States of America
by
Amazon.com

"I would celebrate the Holy Communion service in my pajamas if I thought it would help someone to find faith."

- The Rev. Nicolas Stacey
Sometime Rector of Woolwich

# TABLE OF CONTENTS

# TABLE OF ILLUSTRATIONS

# PREFACE

THIS little book came about at the request of several friends who have heard me lecture on this subject. Although one may be reluctant to think of church vestments as costume, the reality is that all costume is clothing and all clothing is costume.

The difference, when it comes to church vestments, is that these are clothes that are set aside for sacred use. Dorothy Sayers, in her play *The Zeal of Thy House*[i], has St. Michael say,

> *For every work of creation is threefold, an earthly trinity to match the heavenly.*
>
> *First, there is the Creative Idea, passionless, timeless, beholding the whole work complete at once, the end in the beginning: and this is the image of the Father.*
>
> *Second, there is the Creative Energy begotten of that idea, working in time from the beginning to the end, with sweat and passion, being incarnate in the bond of matter: and this is the image of the Word.*
>
> *Third, there is the Creative Power, the meaning of the work and its response to the lively soul: and this is the image of the indwelling Spirit.*
>
> *And these three are one, each equally in itself the whole work, whereof none can exist without the other: and this is the image of the Trinity.*

So it is that one approaches vestment making as sacred work. The Church has long ago come to realize that vestments add a visual footnote to the onward march of the Christian year. And not that only, but as a reminder that priest and people alike are involved in a sacred act. And that is true not only of the wearing of vesture, but of making it, too.

Ms. Sayers again:

> *"… work must be good work before it can call itself God's work."*[ii]

Let us approach our vestment making with the sacredness of the task clearly in mind. Then, when the last stitch is sewn, we may truly say, "All things come of thee, O Lord; and of thine own have we given thee."

Atlanta, Georgia
St. Ambrose's Day, 2007

# DEDICATION
To my good friend and fellow verger
Bruce Garner

# PECULIAR

**pe•cu•liar** / *adj.* **1** strange; odd; unusual (*a peculiar flavor; it is a little peculiar*). **2a** (usu. foll. by *to*) belonging exclusively (*a fashion peculiar to the time*). **b** belonging to the individual (*in their own peculiar way*). **3** particular; special (*a point of peculiar interest*).

-     The Oxford Dictionary, 1998

*The Beretta*
*A hat peculiar to the Clergy*

# IN THE BEGINNING

*When the woman saw that the fruit of the tree was good to eat, and that it was pleasing to the eye and tempting to contemplate, she took some and ate it. She also gave her husband some and he ate it. Then the eyes of both of them were opened and they discovered that they were naked; so they stitched fig leaves together and made themselves loincloths.[iii]*

THE first and foremost thing to say about church vestments is this: they are clothes. Clothes for a specific purpose, certainly, and about which there has been endless discussion, controversy, and in the past at least, even violence. Nevertheless, they are clothes, and that is how their developmental history will be treated in this little book.

Let us say that a television drama opens on an elegantly appointed drawing room in a huge English manor house. A door opens and a woman enters. She is attired in a simple black dress, over which she wears a small white apron. A small white cap is perched on her head.

Unless we are badly mistaken, this person is the maid. However, if the hem of the dress stops at mid-thigh and she is wearing mesh hose and high heels, it is probable that she is a somewhat different kind of maid.

And, without a word being spoken we already know a great deal about this particular character and what role she is likely to play in the next hour or two.

- 15 -

Her clothing, like all clothing, serves three basic purposes. First, it is utilitarian; second, it is ornamental; and third, it proclaims social rank.

**Utility.** Covering up human nakedness is the most obvious kind of utility that clothing offers. Through the centuries how much of what gets covered is quite another matter, and dependent upon the customs of time and place as we shall see. But the utility of clothing extends far beyond the generally essential loincloth or its current equivalent.

*The Ubiqutous Poncho.*

Protection from the elements and the hazards of the workplace are another kind of utility not to be overlooked.

Among such garments, the poncho is probably the most enduring. It appears in almost every culture in one form or another.

This *paenula* of Roman times survives to this day in the form of the *serape*. Fabricated then and now from tightly woven wool, still impregnated with natural lanolin oils, it offers both warmth and shelter from the rain.

The shepherds who watched their flocks that holy springtime night on the hillsides near Bethlehem probably wore a such a garment, as do members of the modern-day military who shelter under plastic ones.

The endurance of this humble garment is not difficult to understand. In its most simple form, it is just a square or rectangle of material with a hole in the center. Then and now, hoods might be added or worn separately; but it takes little skill or imagination to make a very useful basic one.

On the other hand, considerable skill is required to fabricate protective gear for highly specialized jobs.

*American Firefighter's protective hat*

The firefighter's hat, for example, sports an elongated brim at the back to channel water away from the wearer's neck. And, the helmet itself offers protection from falling debris and flying embers.

But, whatever the simplicity or complexity of a particular item of apparel, utility is almost always the original reason for making it.

**Ornament.** Throughout history, when leisure and money were to be had, people have used clothing as a means of personal adornment. The principal reasons for doing so, may be to attract a mate, or to exhibit wealth, or as a symbol of power.

*Stage Costume for the French Maid*

Opposite utility on the clothing spectrum, lie articles of clothing that swath the wearer in huge amounts of fabric in intentional ostentatious display; or in this case, fur:

Stage and screen actress Mae West once made a grand entrance at a Hollywood party, dragging a full-length white fox fur cape on the floor behind her.

"Goodness!" exclaimed her hostess.[iv]

"Goodness had nothing to do with it," Miss West replied.

And, of course, it didn't. The mistress of the double entendre made a fortune by being very good at being bad. To that end, her lavish wardrobe, designed to corset her trademark body shape, was a significant asset.

Clothing that is worn for ornamental purposes, may or may not have much utilitarian value. That is certainly the case for the French Maid character mentioned earlier. Her costume is not so nearly as much utilitarian as it is ornamental and intended to suggest sexuality of a certain sort.

When considering ornament as a motive for human attire, it is impossible to overlook the use of precious metals and jewels.

Of these, the ultimate power symbol is the royal crown, combining as it does, wealth, ostentatious display, and symbolic authority.

**Episcopal Jewels.** Perhaps less awe-inspiring, but highly symbolic nevertheless, are the jewels customarily given a bishop at the time of consecration.

A Pectoral Cross and Ring are the Bishop's traditional jewels.

Royal purple amethysts combine with gold as symbols of membership in the Church's own royalty: princely servants of the Lord of Lords and King of Kings.

**Social Status.** Of course, a royal crown is also the ultimate statement of social status. And other kinds of headgear denote other kinds of status as well.

In occupations secular and sacred, how the head is covered, and how much hair shows, if any, all have much to do with how the social status of the wearer is perceived.

*Royal Chef's Hat*

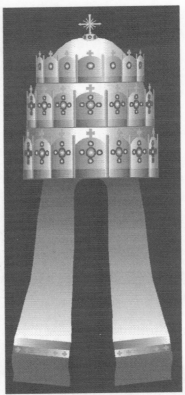

*The Papal Triple Tiara*

Both the royal chef's hat and the Papal Tiara are crowning glories in their own right.

Of the two, the Tiara is a striking symbol of the supreme power of the Papacy. Christ's Vicar on Earth, it might be argued, is deserving of such splendor. What cannot be denied is the Tiara's absolute lack of utility of any sort. Of late, it has not been worn and reposes, for the present, in the Vatican treasury as a precious relic of the past.

On the other hand, besides being a symbol of authority, the royal chef's hat is actually useful. It keeps hair out of the sauces, and its height allows lesser workers to locate the chef quickly and easily in a crowded and busy kitchen.

Other, more mundane and obvious articles of clothing that denote social status include military and police uniforms, nurse's outfits, and the protective clothing worn by industrial workers of various sorts.

Less obvious, perhaps, but just as important, are the coats and ties worn by men in various professional[v] positions. Women, who have come more recently into the professions, have yet to adopt similar symbols of professional status. This may help to explain why the glass ceiling still exists in many places. Symbols are powerful things, and those who lack them are apt to be taken less seriously than those who do.

Over the last two thousand years, the Church has developed peculiar dress as symbols of authority for leaders in the liturgies of worship.

The Church's peculiar dress may also explain why women have entered the priesthood with less difficulty than might otherwise have been the case. The Church's vestments, as symbols of authority are —and have always been— deliberately androgynous.

How and why this came to be we shall shortly discover.

# IMPERIAL ROME

TWO thousand years ago, the Mediterranean Basin was dominated by the Roman Empire, but not exclusively so. The cultural influences of Greece and Egypt also played important parts in the daily lives of Roman citizens as well as those peoples they subjugated to serve them.

The basic garment of the time, worn by both men and women, was the *chiton* or *tunica*. It consisted of two panels of fabric, fastened together on either side of the wearer's neck and above the arms. It was secured about the waist with a cord.

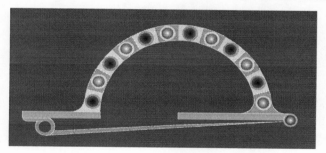

*The Roman fibulae served both as a fastener for garments and as a brooch. This side view shows how it was also the forerunner of the modern safety pin.*

Because the tunica was essentially a loosely fitting garment, it could be gathered onto the body in a variety of ways. It was also made in a variety of lengths. The leisure classes could afford better ones made from fine fabrics. These were generally Egyptian cotton or linen, or a blend of the two.

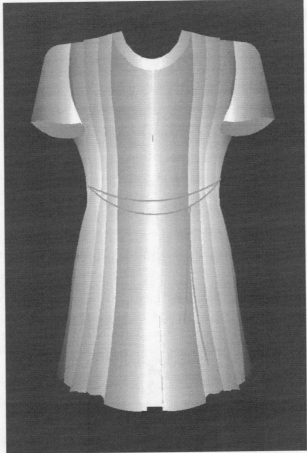

*The Roman tunica was the basic clothing for all classes*

Women generally wore longer ones, which were often folded over at the top to form a peplum. For women, the tie was usually arranged to begin at the back of the neck and cross between the breasts to emphasize their shape: it can be thought of as the original cross-your-heart brassiere.

Artisans, slaves, and craftsmen wore abbreviated and more coarsely woven version of the garment.

When additional clothing was desired, a cloak made from a simple square of fabric was utilized. The *lacerna* (in Greek, *himation*) could be worn over the tunic in a variety of ways, depending upon the amount of protection needed.

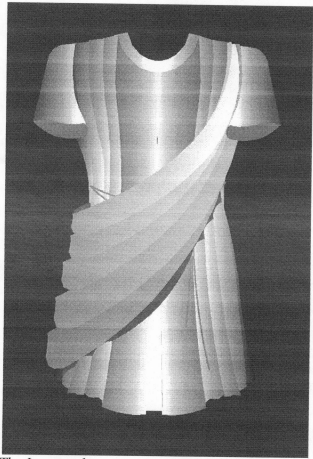

*The Lacerna shown worn open over a tunica. These probably the two garments that are most often pictured in those church windows that depict Jesus and his followers.*

It is to this garment that Jesus probably refers when he says, *"If a man demands your cloak, give him your shirt* [tunica] *also."* And that, of course, would leave the former owner quite naked.

Another garment that figures largely in Greco-Roman attire is the toga. Unlike the humble garments discussed so far, only Roman citizens were permitted to wear the toga.

Among Jesus' earliest followers, it would have been Paul, who as a Roman citizen was entitled to don this elegant, formal and almost totally useless garment.

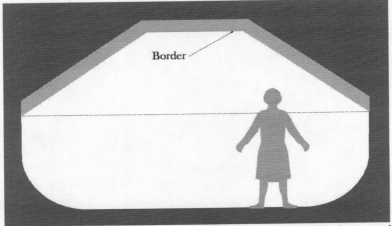

*A toga laid out flat compared to the size of the wearer. The horizontal line shows where the garment is to be folded before wrapping. There were several different kinds of this very formal garment.[vi]*

The toga was made from a huge piece of fabric—often as much as nine yards long. It was at least as 1.5 times as tall as the wearer, and when wrapped in place, the left arm was so restricted in movement as to be essentially useless.

And, finally, all classes in really foul weather utilized the poncho-like, previously described *paenula*.

It must be said that nudity, or at least near-nudity, was not uncommon at this time. Like the French Maid costume of bedroom-farce fame, clothing was utilized as much for its peek-a-boo sex appeal as it was for utility. Socialization in the baths was essentially a nude activity. Sports were usually played nude, and the athletic contests of the early Olympic games were conducted in the buff.

Of course there were occasions when more modest dress was appropriate, such as in the Senate, or when visiting a temple, unless a sexual offering was to be made.

In Egypt, farther south and warmer, clothing was even more diaphanous and/or optional.

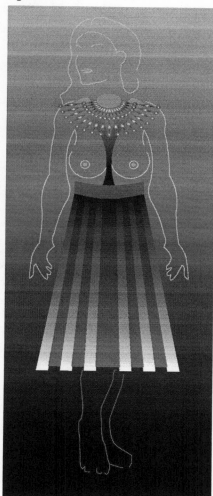

If Cleopatra displayed her physical charms to both Caesar and Mark Anthony in an Egyptian suspender dress, such as the one illustrated at left, it is small wonder that she became a political power and a scandal in Rome.

Here, again, is an example of the use of clothing primarily for ornamentation and as sexual display.

But sexual display and semi-nudity were not universal throughout the Empire.

Among the subjugated people were the Jews, who were looked upon as quite strange by the average Roman.

First of all, they believed in a single invisible God. The Romans were willing to give them some latitude with this peculiarity, since their religion was a very old one. In fact, it was so respected that they were even excused from making a sacrifice of incense to the genius of the Emperor.

And, also in keeping with Imperial policy, worship continued at the Temple in Jerusalem, Albeit under the watchful eyes of Roman Guards. So it is informative to contrast the secular garb of the Roman Empire with what the High Priest wore at the Temple.

His outer vestment, complete with golden bells and pomegranates around the hem, is worn over a tunica-like garment. But look at the difference: the High Priest's tunica has full-length sleeves and the hem extends all the way to the floor.

Nor were his vestments at odds with everyday Jewish dress. His outerwear certainly set him apart in terms of office and authority. However, this overall sense of modest dress permeated Jewish life and culture.

Indeed, it permeates most of the Middle East to this day. One only has to watch the evening news or read current news magazines to be aware of the veil, the burka and the burnoose.

It is probable that the Jews of Jesus' day looked upon the pagan Romans with as much distain for their sartorial excesses as do the more conservative peoples of the Middle East regard westerners today.

The ascendancy of Christianity and the ultimate disintegration of the Roman Empire brought about huge cultural changes. The modest dress of the Jews, who were the first Christians, was ultimately adopted throughout the Holy Roman Empire.

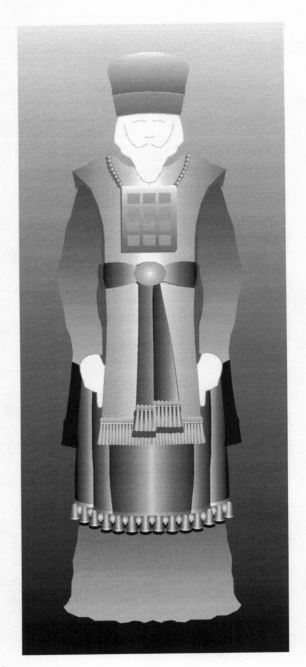

And the expansion of Christianity into the colder climate of northern Europe brought about the need to adopt warmer clothing as well.

Out of these changes comes a blend of the requirement for modest dress, coupled with the adaptation of Roman patterns of clothing. These changes result in an evolution of everyday garments. And all of these factors influenced the Eucharistic vestments as well. Although they have changed in cut and ornamentation over the centuries, the basic garments have remained essentially the same.

It is also easy to see how the humble *paenula* became the Chasuble.

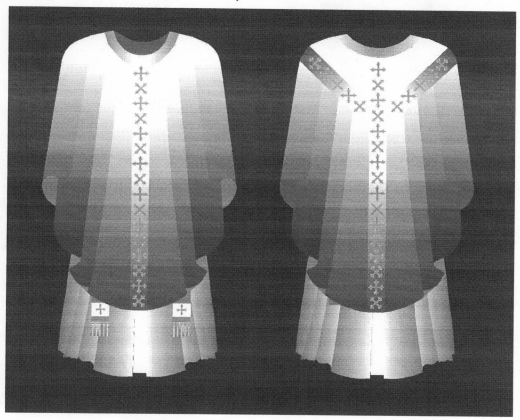

*(L) Contemporary Alb, Stole and Chasuble (R) Back of the Chasuble,*

It is easy to see how the tunica developed into the Alb. It is simply the same garment, although now with long T-shaped sleeves and a hem reaching to the ankles. It derives its new name from its white color, which represents the robes of the redeemed after they have been washed in the blood of the Lamb.

But, where did the stole come from? The best answer is that nobody knows. Several different ideas have been suggested. Perhaps it can be traced back to a liturgical napkin[vii] or to a folded neck-cloth worn by the priest. It was introduced, in the fourth century, in the Eastern Church and then migrated to the West.

*A Stole. All ornamentation is optional, save for the traditional cross placed at center back cross.*

# THE MIDDLE AGES

WHEN Constantine moved the capitol of the Holy Roman Empire to the East, there was a general disintegration of imperial control in the West. From a political perspective, what control there was came largely from the Church, which stepped in to fill the vacuum. Thereupon, it took upon itself the trappings of earthly power. The use of ornamentation as a symbol of power was soon seen in the previously humble vesture of the Church.

And, in spite of what is often called the "Dark Ages," Christianity spread northwards, taking root in Ireland in particular. Monasticism in the West can be dated from about 340, when St. Athanasius visited Rome accompanied by two monks from what we would now call the Coptic Church. Many felt called to a life of work, contemplation and prayer. Life was hard and short for the average person.

Monasticism offered, in exchange for vows of poverty, chastity and obedience, the assurance of shelter and a decent diet. Worshiping at set hours of the day and night inspired the writing of various liturgies. Members of the monastic communities stopped work or arose from sleep at all hours for the all-important work of worship.

Arising nightly from the relative warmth of one's bed at three o'clock in the morning, for the sole purpose of singing the office of Lauds in an unheated church, in the north of England in January, requires considerable self-discipline and could rightly be called work.

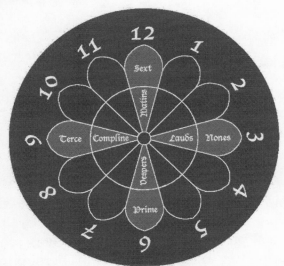

*One version of the Monastic Hours, with eight different services in twenty-four hours.*

Monastic attire of the Middle Ages varied from one order to the next, and through the centuries. But the basics were the same. The undergarment is still the *tunica*, with long sleeves and reaching to the floor; and now called the *chemise*. Over the *chemise* monks of the Monastery of St. Genesius-in-the-Glen[viii] would have worn a robe or tunic.

This simple outer garment becomes, in our own time, the academic Gown. It is full and flowing, with large sleeves. And, at least in winter, the robe was often lined with fur for the sake of additional warmth. Such a garment was called a *pellice*.

At the insistent ringing of the chapel bell, the monks would arise, throw a robe on over their *chemise*, wrap a woolen scarf about their necks, and step out into the cloister to face the cold.

Members of monastic orders are supposed to be otherworldly. But, the sin of vanity can creep in anywhere. In certain quarters there arose some contention over who should wear the finest of the *pellices*. The bishop put an end to the quarreling by decreeing that a plain white linen Gown was to be worn over the robes; *i.e.,* "*sur pellice*," and so the Surplice was born.

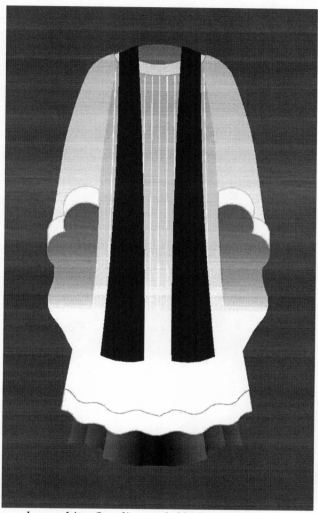

*A modern white Surplice and black tippet worn over a Cassock. This is the appropriate vesture for the choir offices.*

The tippet followed thereafter, derived from the woolen scarf worn originally for warmth[ix]. So it was that the first two of the vestments for the choir offices came into being, but the robe remained.

**Other Eucharistic Vestments**. In the fourth century, the Dalmatic came into use as a vestment for the Deacon. And by the sixth century, the Tunical had been added for the sub-deacon.

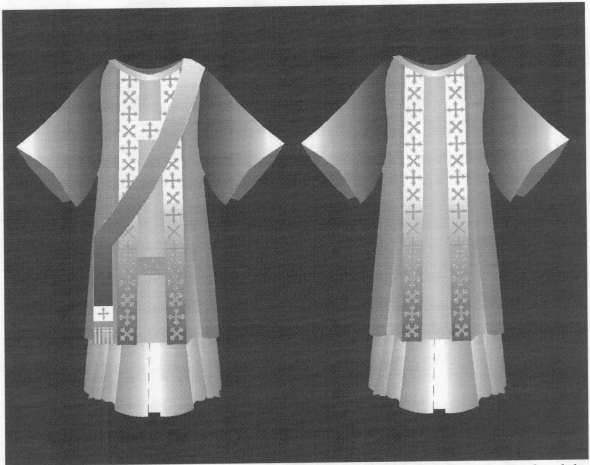

*Dalmatic (L) and Tunical (R). The only distinction is that the Tunical is less richly ornamented, and the Deacon wears a Stole over one shoulder. Sleeves may be open or stitched closed along the bottom. Ornamentation varies.*

**Cope**. The Cope can be said to be as ancient the Chasuble. Or it can be said as truthfully the other way around, since they both begin as the same garment. The essential difference between them is that the Chasuble did not open up the front but the Cope version did. They were used interchangeably until the Cope expanded into a much larger garment later in the medieval period.

*A Cope of modern cut, worn over a modern Cassock-Alb.*

*The same Cope as on the preceding page, as seen from the back.*

It is during this time that the Church begins to mandate distinctive attire for members of the clergy. For a time, the Cope becomes that distinctive garment, made from a plain, dark colored fabric and reaching at least to the shins.

However, with time, the Cope developed into one of the Church's most sumptuous garments.

Although usually associated primarily with the ceremonial attire of a bishop, a Cope may properly be worn by any minister, lay or ordained.

**Mitre.** The first mentions of the bishops' Mitre occur around the year 1,000. And the very first illustration shows something not unlike the headgear of the High Priest at the Temple in Jerusalem. It looks something like and upside-down sack and appears to have a drawstring around the bottom These presumably would have been used to fit it to the wearer's head.

Its origins are uncertain, but it is likely that the drawstrings (if that's what they are) developed eventually into the two lappets that hang down the back of the Mitre.

At some point, it developed a bifurcated form in the western Church, and was first worn with the division running front-to-back.

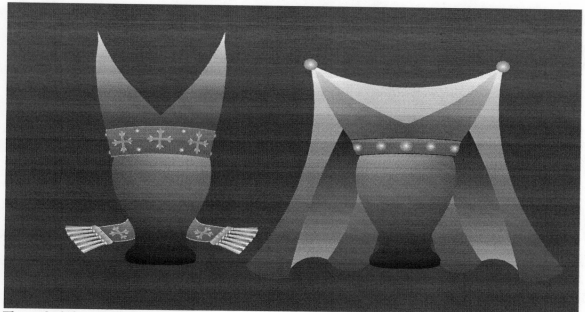

*The early bifurcated Mitre may be only somewhat less silly-looking when compared to a lady's horned headdress of the high middle ages.*

Perhaps an unbecoming analogy was the reason that the Mitre was soon worn the way we see it now, with the division running side-to-side.

What is certain is that it has retained more of its original shape in the East and became bifurcated only in the West.

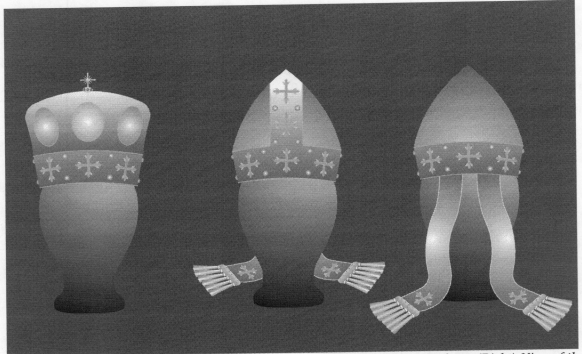

*(Left) An Eastern Orthodox Mitre. (Center) A Western Mitre as seen from the front. (Right) View of the Western Mitre from the back.*

The bifurcated shape is intended to represent the flames that alighted upon the heads of the disciples at Pentecost. The lappets, it is said, represent the law and the prophets.

**The Crozier.** Although not a garment in any sense of the word, the Crozier is an item of such importance that a bishop (within jurisdiction[x]) would be liturgically ill equipped without one.

The English word Crozier comes from the French word *crosse* for this item.

In modern times, Croziers are to be found in many shapes, both traditional and modern, but all mimic in some way the shepherds crook upon which they are based.

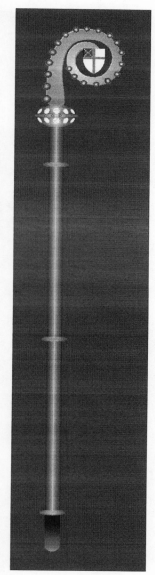

It is not unknown for modern bishops to be searched extensively at airports in the belief they are carrying a dangerous weapon. And perhaps they are.[xi]

**The Investiture Controversy.** In the Middle Ages, bishops and archbishops, abbots and abbesses, were persons of both ecclesiastical and temporal power. Thus, they were often called upon to serve two masters.

Papal authority wanted to bestow the symbols of Church office to those in authority. The monarchs of Europe wanted fealty. The arrangement in England, confirmed in Magna Carta, was that the Pope or his representative could vest the symbols in those persons freely elected in England by the Church in England, without interference from either Pope or King. But this struggle for ultimate power was destined to continue well into the Renaissance.

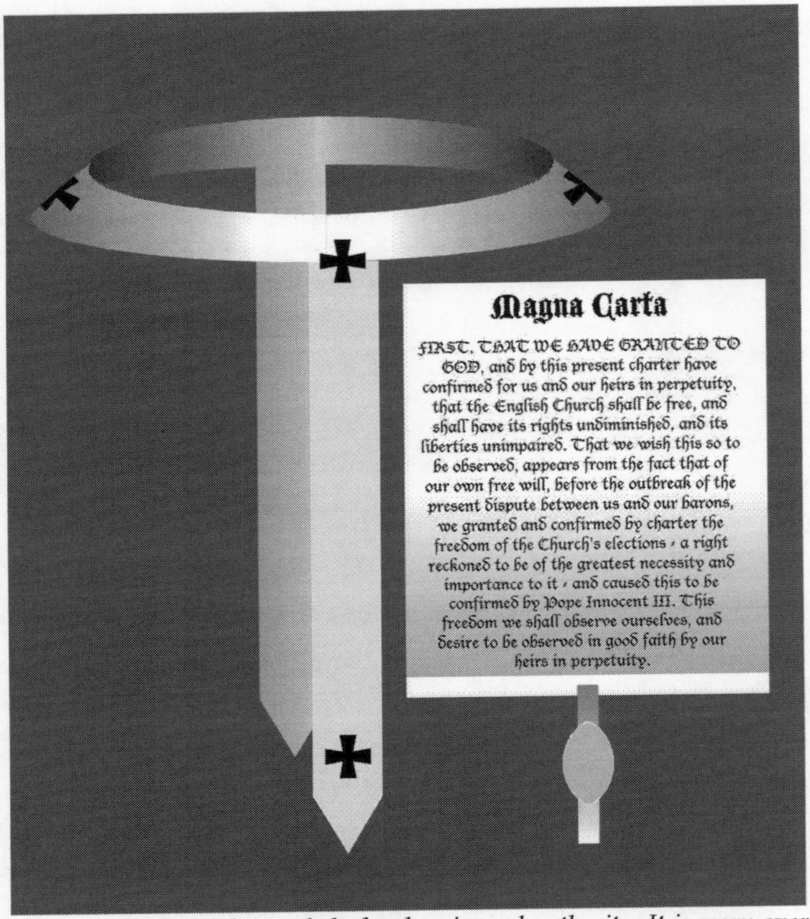
Magna Carta
FIRST, THAT WE HAVE GRANTED TO GOD, and by this present charter have confirmed for us and our heirs in perpetuity, that the English Church shall be free, and shall have its rights undiminished, and its liberties unimpaired. That we wish this so to be observed, appears from the fact that of our own free will, before the outbreak of the present dispute between us and our barons, we granted and confirmed by charter the freedom of the Church's elections - a right reckoned to be of the greatest necessity and importance to it - and caused this to be confirmed by Pope Innocent III. This freedom we shall observe ourselves, and desire to be observed in good faith by our heirs in perpetuity.

*The Pallium (L) is the symbol of arch-episcopal authority. It is worn over the shoulders with the tabs hanging down in front and in back. They are unknown in the democratically governed American church, because it does not have archbishops.*

By the end of the Middle Ages, almost all of the vesture that we associate with the Episcopal Church had come into being. But not all; the changes of the Renaissance were blowing in the wind.

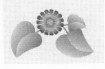

# OH! THOSE TUDORS!

THE Renaissance brought about many striking changes in the Western world. But amidst the many changes, Henry VIII did **not** start either the Church *in* England, nor the Church *of* England.

The Church *in* England was founded, centuries earlier by St. Columba, a follower of St. Patrick. In 337, bishops of the Church in England were present at an ecumenical council in Arles, France. The Sarum[xii] Rite was well established and continued in use until Cranmer's Prayer Book of 1549.

Of the intricacies of the Sarum Rite, Archbishop Cranmer complained:

> *"... the number and hardness of the rules called the pie, and the manifold changings of the service, was the cause, yet to turn the book only, was so hard and intricate a matter, that many times, there was more business to find out what should be read, then to read it when it was found out."*

Of the Sarum Use of color, we shall have more to discover presently.

As for Henry, he didn't start the Church *of* England, either. In fact he vigorously suppressed any and all Protestant reformation efforts. What he did do, as a result of his dissolution of the monasteries, the intricacies of his six marriages, and having himself declared Supreme Governor of the Church in England, was to set in motion political forces that could not be stopped.

*Henry VIII, taken from a contemporary painting of that monarch. His perfect gentleman's attire includes a codpiece that protrudes from the skirt of his doublet.*

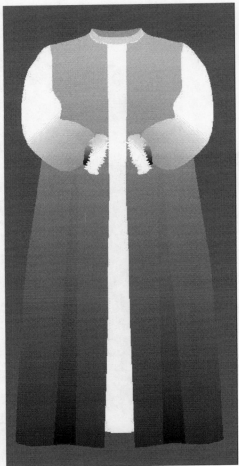

*The Rochet (white) and Chimere (red) are the proper choir vesture for Anglican bishops. Red wristbands gather the sleeves of the Rochet. The fullness of the Chimere is gathered across the back in cartridge pleats.*[xiii]

Henry, like all mortals died and was buried – in a Roman Catholic rite by Roman Catholic prelates. Political differences with the Pope notwithstanding, Henry had been named by the Pope *Defender of the Faith,* and so he remained. It is a title used even today by the monarchs of England, and perhaps not without some irony.

Henry's son Edward VI became king at age nine, and his protestant counselors caused the introduction of the first Book of Common Prayer in 1549, and a second one in 1552, just before Edward's death in 1553. In pertinent part, the 1552 rubrics say:

> ... *the minister at the time of the Communion and all other times in his ministration shall use neither Albe, vestment, nor Cope; but being archbishop or bishop, he shall have and wear a rochet; and being a preest or deacon, he shall have and wear a Surplice onely.*

So, Roman Catholic vestments were burned, or stored, or hidden away and services became plain, simple and in a language "understanded of the people."

Edward VI's short time on the throne was followed by the reign of Henry's maniacally devoted Roman Catholic Daughter Mary, who had Archbishop Cranmer burned alive for having produced Edward's prayer book. And she didn't stop there, either. She didn't get her sobriquet *Bloody* for nothing.

Mary's only rival, and the hope of the reformationists, was her younger half-sister Elizabeth. Mary had Elizabeth imprisoned in the Tower of London. Here her inquisitors wanted to know if Elizabeth believed in the Real Presence.[xiv]

To say, "yes," would save her life and loose her protestant support. To say, "no," would lead her to the block or the stake. Elizabeth was intelligent, wise, and witty.  In her cell, she penned her answer:

> *He was the Word that spake it,*
> *and what that Word doth make it,*
> *I do believe and take it.*

After Mary's death from an abdominal tumor, Elizabeth finally came to the throne in 1558. In 1559, the Elizabethan Settlement placed power over the church firmly in the hands of the monarch:

> ... *the Queen's Highness is the only Supream Governor of this Realm, and of all other her Highness Dominions and Countries, as well in all Spiritual or Ecclesiastical Things or Causes, as Temporal; and that no foreign Prince, Person, Prelate State or Potentate, hath or ought to have any Jurisdiction, Power, Superiority, Preheminence, or Authority Ecclesiastical or Spiritual, within this Realm ...*

*The modern, double-breasted Anglican Cassock, with its deep cuffs and fringed cincture, differs considerably from its Roman Catholic counterpart. It is black, except for cathedral use, which is purple.*

Of course, the Renaissance was not just about the Reformation. There were many other striking changes in the world. Among these was the development of clothing that, for the first time since the Roman Empire, was intended to enhance the appearance of the human body. But unlike the simple drapery of the past, Renaissance clothing heralds the beginning of modern tailoring.

The Renaissance also heralds the point at which, generally speaking, Church vestment design remains based on the overall pattern of the Middle Ages, while contemporary clothing styles continue to change.

It was during this period that the Cassock emerged in various forms. It replaced the medieval robe and, at the same time, retained the long skirt associated with clerical modesty. The cut of a Cassock is very much like the pattern for a man's coat. It is essentially flat in front with fullness in the back, by means of large flat pleats over the hips and center back.

As the Cassock replaced the robe as the standard clerical garment, so it also became the basic garment for the choir offices and eventually including the choristers as well.

The notched, upright Cassock collar was originally worn over the ordinary white shirt that developed from the *chemise*. This garment had a fold-down collar and a neck-scarf (usually silk). This form of gentlemen's wear existed well into the mid-nineteenth century.[xv] Thus, one saw the black Cassock and notched collar with a band of white above it.

But it is not until the invention of the detachable collar, about 1850, that the clerical collar comes into being. Shirts began to be manufactured without collars, the idea being that the shirt could be worn several times, with a freshly washed and starched collar (and sometimes cuffs) each day.

With this development, it became easy to simply reverse the collar and fasten it in the back. This continued the unbroken look of the previous shirt collar and tie, but with a more finished, tailored look.

By the end of the nineteenth century, the reversed collar is standard attire. The Cassock begins to disappear as street wear, and a black clerical suit, with black vest-front and collar replaced it.

However, the Cassock continued to be worn indoors and as the foundation garment for the Eucharistic vestments until near the end of the twentieth century. Over it was worn the old-style tunic-shaped Alb with a detached hood-like amice.

All three have now been replaced at the Eucharist by the current Cassock-Alb, made of heavier fabric, with a skirt cut more like a Cassock skirt and a stand-up collar which is all that remains of the amice. However, the Cassock remains the basic garment for the choir offices.

# THE OXFORD MOVEMENT

THE distinctive, plain vesture and simple services of the Church of England remained very much the same from the sixteenth to the nineteenth centuries. The churches in the United States, and throughout the British Empire followed this example.

In 1833 Anglican clergymen at the University of Oxford (the "tractarians") sought to renew the Church of England by reviving certain Roman Catholic doctrines and rituals.

Known as the Oxford Movement, the tractarians exerted a great influence, doctrinally, spiritually, and liturgically not only on the Church of England but also throughout the Anglican Communion.

The Oxford movement stressed higher standards of worship, and particularly in the later period many changes were made in the church services. These included the beautification of churches, wearing the ancient "Catholic" vestments, and emphasis on hymn singing, chant, and choral music.

But every effort to revive ceremonial customs also aroused a storm of excitement and opposition leading at times to rioting.

Introduced by the Archbishop of Canterbury, the 1874 Public Worship Regulation Act was passed by Parliament. It's intention was to forbid "ritualism and Catholic worship."

The Oxford Movement churchmen resisted the intrusion of Parliament into spiritual affairs. By the end of the nineteenth century, prohibition against the use of vestments, "high church" ritual and chant was largely ignored. The Act was repealed, not without continuing controversy, in 1965.

As a result, the forms of worship we know today, and the various vestments associated with worship are, like the Church itself, both catholic and protestant, orthodox and reformed.

# STAGE AND SCREEN COSTUME

ONE of any costumer designer's worst nightmares is doing something inappropriate or incorrect. There is almost always somebody in the audience who is an expert on any subject. And when a costume is "wrong," it becomes a distraction for them. It also can make the costume designer and the production look pretty silly.

Of course, good costume design can – and often should – take liberties with reality in the interests of presenting the playwright's world. But those liberties should always be undertaken based in knowledge of the subject matter.

Herewith is basic information about who wears what and when they wear it.

**The Christian Year.** Beginning in the Early Gothic period, until the present, the Church has maintained a calendar that is separate from the secular world. It is divided into these Seasons:

- Advent – the four Sundays, and intervening weekdays before Christmas. (Blue or Violet)

- Christmas – twelve days long, beginning on December 25. Epiphany, the visit of the Wise Men occurs on the twelfth day. (White)

- Post Epiphany – a season of variable length, depending upon the date of Easter Day. (Green)

- Lent – a period of 40 days devoted to penitence. (Violet)

- Easter – a period of 50 days of rejoicing, ending with the Feast of Pentecost. (White, but Pentecost is Red.)

- Post Pentecost, a season of variable length, depending upon the date of Easter Day. (Green)

For more information on the use of liturgical colors, see the chart for the Use of Sarum and associated commentary.

The two events that are most likely to occur in playscripts are weddings and funerals. What is worn depends upon whether there is a celebration of the Mass or Holy Communion. This would be very unusual in a play, but it might be possible to infer that it will follow the scene in which the wedding or funeral takes place.

Prior to the Oxford Movement, this possibility is quite unlikely. Afterwards, much more so. After 1967, it would be almost certain.

When a Mass or Holy Communion is to follow a wedding or funeral, the vestments for the Eucharist would be worn. For a wedding, the color is always white. For a funeral prior to 1967, the color is violet. After 1967 it is white.

Otherwise, the vestments are the Office vestments: Cassock, and Surplice worn with a Stole rather than a tippet. For weddings, the Stole is white. For a funeral prior to 1967, the Stole is violet. After 1967 is white. These same vestments are also worn at graveside for the burial. In inclement weather, a cemetery cloak may be added. It is a full-circle cloak of heavy wool, reaching to mid ankle, and fastened in front with either a chain clasp or an agriffe.

**Lay Assistants.** The most common kind of lay assistant a costumer is likely to encounter is an acolyte. Originally, "altar boys," this lay office is now filled in most places by both sexes, who may be adults or children. They wear either an Alb, or Cassock and Surplice. Children sometimes wear a cotta instead of a Surplice. It is essentially the same garment as a Surplice, but shorter in length.

The body reaches just to the point of the hip, and the sleeves are hemmed level with the waist.

**Ordained Clergy.** There are three orders, ascending in rank thus: deacon, priest and bishop.

Deacons. Generally speaking, deacons are on their way to becoming priests and serve as assistants to a priest until they have practical experience with priestly duties.. They do not celebrate mass or pronounce blessings.

Priests are either the rectors of churches, assistants to rectors, vicars assigned to churches or missions, canons in cathedrals, or sometimes archdeacons.

Bishops are in charge of a diocese; a group of congregations in a specific geographic area. The congregations may be churches, missions, monastic houses, and/or hospitals. Some, but not all, Anglican clergy wear a berretta. It is appropriate for both outdoor and indoor wear. However, it is always removed for prayers. This can get to be too busy in dramatic action, so choose carefully.

Bishops wear a fairly wide variety of garments, specifically:

- The default costume is Rochet and Chemere, worn with a black tippet. The foundation garment below these is a Cassock and collar. The Cassock may be either red or violet.

- To the Rochet and Chemere, one may add Cope and Mitre. The Crozier may or may not also be appropriate. (see endnotes). Cope and Mitre may be of about any color. White, gold and red are probably the most usual. In practice, black is not used, but could be an interesting departure if the script calls for a very dark interpretation of the bishop's office.

- If the bishop were celebrating the Mass or Holy Communion, the Eucharistic vestments would be worn with the Mitre added. However, Mitre is not worn while the bishop is actually at the altar. It is put on again at the end of the service before pronouncing the blessing.

None of these garments above would be worn except for a church service.

**Street Wear.** From earlier times until about 1935-1940, a robe, and later on a Cassock and collar would have been worn in public or in the church offices.

Thereafter, the Cassock was gradually replaced by a black clerical suit with a black vest-front (a Rabat) that features a notched, upright collar like that one on a Cassock. It is worn with a reversed collar. Beginning in the 1970s, clergy attire became much more relaxed. The Rabat disappears in favor of shirts, either gray or black, with a reversed collar. A bishop's shirt is usually red, although some bishops prefer violet. Women priests dress in the same general fashion; usually with a skirt, but slacks are not unknown.

**Monastic Attire.** Every monastic order, male and female, has its own set of peculiar vesture. Research in this area is imperative., if a proper representation of a given order is to be accomplished. But if a generic representation is needed, the following will generally suffice.

- A Gown is the foundation garment. The cut is the same as for a Cassock, but with much more generous, tube-like sleeves. It should be possible for the actor to cross his/her arms inside the sleeves.

- The Gown is covered by a Scapular (see pattern below).

- Over Gown and Scapular, men wear a chaperon without a lirepipe. Women wear Gorget, Wimple and veil. A short-cut pattern for this appears below as well.

Colors are generally all black, or black with a grey Scapular. Anglican Franciscan monks wear dark brown, overall.

Sandals, with black hose are appropriate wear for either sex, or women may wear stage utility shoes.

Caskets in Episcopal Churches are never open, and are always covered with a pall. It is a rectangle of cloth, often matching the vestments, that covers the casket completely. It can be ornamented with a large cross that runs end-to-end and side-to-side, made from the same kind(s) of trim used on the vestments themselves. It, too, is violet before 1967 and white afterwards.

# MAKING VESTMENTS

I T is not unreasonable to assert that simple vestments, simply made, can be both effective and relatively inexpensive.

But, before addressing the actual fabrication of vestments, it is essential to discuss the process that will be used and the fabrics from which they are to be made.

**Basic Skills.** Basic sewing skills are needed to construct the vestments described in this chapter. If you can cut and sew basic garments, then proceed. If you can't, or haven't, you'll probably need the help of somebody who is more experienced.

**Liturgical Colors.** In the United States, Anglican practice is divided between using the old Sarum Rite colors and following Roman Catholic use.

Basic Colors of the Roman Rite are four: White, Green, Red and Violet. They are used in the same way as in the chart below, except that violet is used in lieu of blue in Advent.[xvi]

Although church buildings of the Middle Ages were aflame with applied color, those same buildings today are generally plain. In time, the old colors have faded away and have not been replaced. However, bright colors continue to be used in church vestments.

# The Use of Sarum

| Color | Used | Notes |
|---|---|---|
| Best | Easter, Christmas and the Octave of Each; Special Events. | May be any color or fabric, but is intended to be unusually rich. |
| White | Festivals, in lieu of Best Set; Saints, other than those martyred; Funerals and Weddings. | Sometimes still used at Holy Baptism. |
| Green | Ordinary days | Ferial days of the week, and in ordinary time after Pentecost and Epiphany |
| Blue | Advent, except for the 3rd Sunday | |
| Violet | Lent, except for the 4th Sunday | And all other Fasts |
| Rose | Third Sunday of Advent and Fourth of Lent | Gaudate and Lautare Sundays respectively |
| Red | Feasts of the Holy Spirit, martyred saints and Ordinations | Any implied reference to blood or fire. |

If the church building where the vestments will be used, or if they are to be personally owned ones, saturated colors should be used. But if the church building is brightly decorated, attention should be paid to how the vestment color(s) will work in such an environment.

For example, the author's parish church has a bright red apse, trimmed in gold and dark blue-green. So, our Lenten set—which should be violet[xvii]—is a considerably lighter, almost lavender color. Saturated violet would tend to look too black against the red background.

**Fabric Selection and Hand.** Begin by picking the fabric and trims that you would like to use for your vestment project.

Church supply houses often sell liturgical fabric and trims by the yard. The advantage to purchasing these goods is that they are always available, whereas other fabrics may be produced for a limited period of time and then go out of production.

The disadvantage is cost. Specially woven liturgical fabrics are produced in relatively small quantities and must be kept in stock for many years. And, church supply houses cannot afford to sell these goods cheaply enough to allow for the amateur vestment-maker to compete successfully with them, using their own products.

Finding suitable, cost-effective fabrics in saturated colors can be difficult. Some sources include the following:

- Vogue Fabrics (www.voguefabricsstore.com) Christian-symbol brocades, orphery bandings and appliqués.

- Rose Brand (www.rosebrand.com).[xviii] Silks, satins and metallics.

- Associated Fabrics Corporation (www.afcnewyork.com). Satins and taffetas.

- Dazian (www.dazian.com). Patterned and plain fabrics that can be searched by color.

Discount and remnant stores in your area or on line are a good source for brocades, damasks and jacquards. These stores usually sell bolt ends at terrific savings, so it is possible to obtain very high-end fabric quite inexpensively.

The fabric you choose should be soft enough to fall in simple, natural folds, and heavy enough to do so naturally without adding artificial weight in the hem of the garment.

Stoles, altar frontals and superfrontals, pulpit antependia and bible bookmarks can be stiff, but soft, flowing Chasubles and Copes cannot. In order to make both kinds of vesture from the same face goods, the pieces that need to be stiffened will need special attention.

You will need 4.5 to 5 yards of face good for a Chasuble and celebrant's Stole. And there will be enough fabric left over for a burse and veil as well. A Dalmatic or tunical will require two and two-thirds yards, and a Cope at least six.

For each yard of face goods, you will also need the same amount of lining fabric. And, if the vestments are to be interlined, you will need interlining, too. There of two kinds of interlining to be considered.

- Soft Interlining. Unless you need to add weight to make the Chasuble or Cope to hang nicely, soft interlining for these garments will probably be unnecessary. That will hold true, so long as the face goods and the lining are about the same color, or when the face goods are opaque. In instances where the color of the lining shows below the face goods, interlining is essential. Otherwise, your scarlet-lined, white- or ivory-colored Chasuble may end up looking pink under bright lighting.

- Stiffening Interlining. Unless the face goods for the Stoles is unusually heavy, it will be a good idea to add an interlining that will add body to the face goods. Either woven or unwoven interlining can be used and the fusible type (that can be ironed in place) is recommended.

Before discussing the matter of trimming vestments, a quick review of basic color theory may be in order.

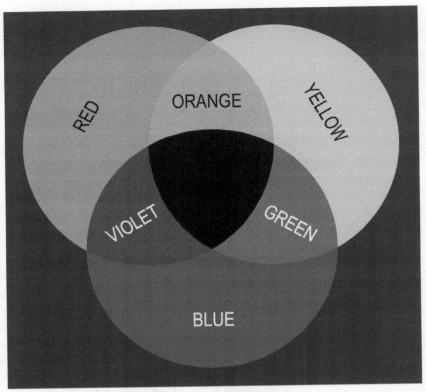

- **Saturated colors** are those colors that cannot be made any stronger.
- Colors to which white has been added to lighten them are **tints** of the basic color.
- Colors to which black has been added to darken them are **shades** of the basic color.
- Colors to which some of the complementary color has been added are **grayed** colors.
- Red, Blue and Yellow are the **primary colors.**
- Violet, Green and Orange are the **secondary colors.**
- Colors adjacent to each other are **analogous colors.**
- Colors are **complimentary colors.**

**Lining and Trim.** Choosing the lining for a vestment is an important aspect of how the finished product will be perceived by the viewer. In smaller spaces, a lining that is **analogous** to face fabric is generally preferable. However, in larger spaces a **complimentary** lining will give the garment more definition when seen from a distance.

Trims should generally be chosen for contrast. **Tints** and **shades** of the fabric will provide less contrast than **compliments.**

Orphery and Galloon. The orphery banding that is used to trim vestments with strips of contrasting color is, in its basic form, simply a ribbon. So, it follows that for the simplest kind of vestment project, a simple three-inch ribbon will do very nicely.

From the middle Ages onwards, ribbons of this type were woven with Christian symbols as a part of the design. These were often woven on small handlooms in limited quantities. Today, there are many kinds of ribbons on the market that include patterns suitable for church as well as secular use.

Careful examination of yard goods may yield another source for orphery bandings. When a suitable pattern is found, it is simply a matter of cutting the fabric into ribbons, joining the lengths, and applying the result to the vestment face.

Galloon is a very narrow ribbon or other flat trim that is used as a cover. It is applied by hand over (a) seams, (b) rough-cut orphery made from yard goods, and (c) where orphery ribbon has been applied by machine stitching.

Appliqué. Basic Christian symbols can be had at reasonable prices, but the proprietary ones offered by church supply houses are pricey. One alternative is to either make your own, or have someone skilled in embroidery make them for you. Another alternative is to cut them from fabric that has been backed with a stiffening interlining.

In the case of all appliqués, it will be necessary to couch[xix] the item in place in order to achieve a finished look.

**Pattern Take-off.** Patterns for vestments are not generally available in the marketplace. There is little call for them, and church supply houses guard their patterns carefully, since they are a part of their trade secrets.

The patterns presented here are very basic ones and are sized for use with commercially available fabrics that are generally between fifty-two and fifty-four inches wide.

Since it is not possible to print full-fixed patterns in this little book, they have been reduced to fit the page. You will need to enlarge them to full size, using the grid method. In order to do this, you will need to use large pieces of paper to make your own full sized pattern.

Wide brown paper or butcher paper is a good choice for this purpose. If you cannot find paper that is at lease fifty-four inches wide, you can fasten narrower strips together using glue or tape.

When you are ready to begin your take-off, iron the paper flat, using a clothes iron on a low setting and with the steam feature turned off.

The squares on the patterns in the next section will vary in size, but they are all four inches "in scale." Just make the squares on your paper four inches each, and then copy the pattern onto the paper using the squares as a guide to position the cutting and stitching lines.

## The Chasuble Pattern

Begin by drawing four-inch squares on your pattern paper and numbering them as shown in the pattern diagram. Then, draw in the pattern lines using the grid as a guide. When you have done that, you will have one-half of the Chasuble pattern.

Fold the pattern paper in half vertically along the centerline of the pattern (line number "1").

Next, use sewing pins to pin the two halves together just inside the outside edge of the pattern line. Trim away both layers of paper, leaving only the pattern itself. **But, don't cut the matching notches just yet.** When you have trimmed away the excess paper, unpin and unfold the paper pattern and set it aside. Repeat the same process with the pattern for the Chasuble back.

When you have cut the Back out, fold the Front and Back pattern pieces together, with the back inside the front. Match them together, aligning the bottom point and the sides. If the curved sides do not match perfectly, use either the front or the back pattern as a guide and trim the other piece until they are alike. Keep the curve as consistent and smooth as you can.

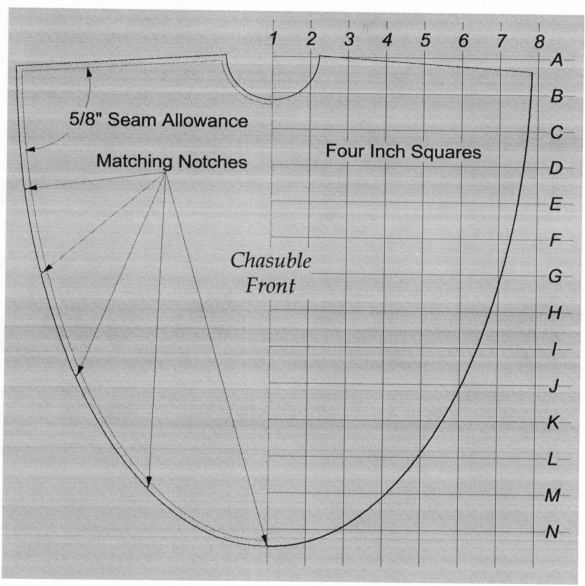

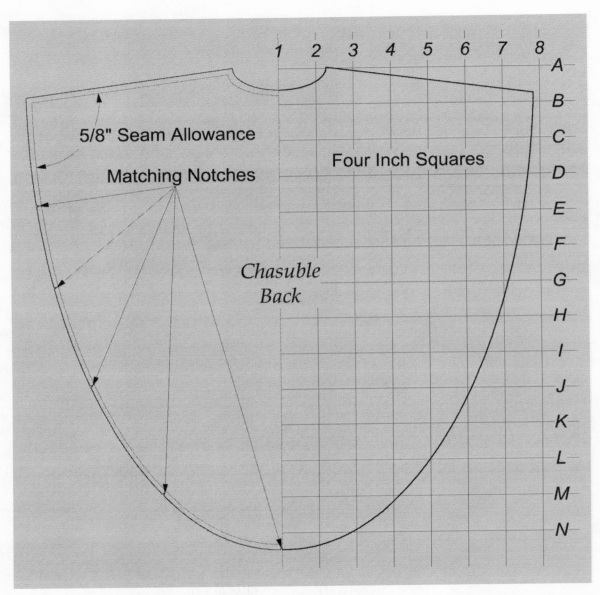

Chasuble Back

5/8" Seam Allowance

Matching Notches

Four Inch Squares

The top shoulder and neck openings will not match each other. This is intentional, so that the shoulder seam will lie more naturally along the top of the wearer's shoulders. Now cut the matching notches and the front and back of the Chasuble pattern are complete.

Next, cut the two pieces of the neck banding from and scraps on either side of the bottom of the Chasuble. The banding is in two pieces, which will be sewn together later. It will form a circular shape about thirty inches long.

After sewing, it will be folded so that there are four thicknesses, each about ¾" wide. It is then applied by hand along the seam line at the neck.

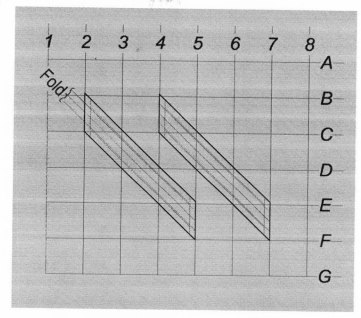

## Dalmatic and Tunical Pattern

Other, items of vesture include the Dalmatic (worn by a deacon) and the Tunical (worn by the sub-deacon). Each of these garments uses the same basic pattern. The difference is that the Dalmatic is more elaborately trimmed than the Tunical.

Taking off the flat pattern is the same as for the Chasuble. The hand-applied neck-binding pattern shown for the Chasuble should also be used to finish the neck opening of Dalmatics and Tunicals.

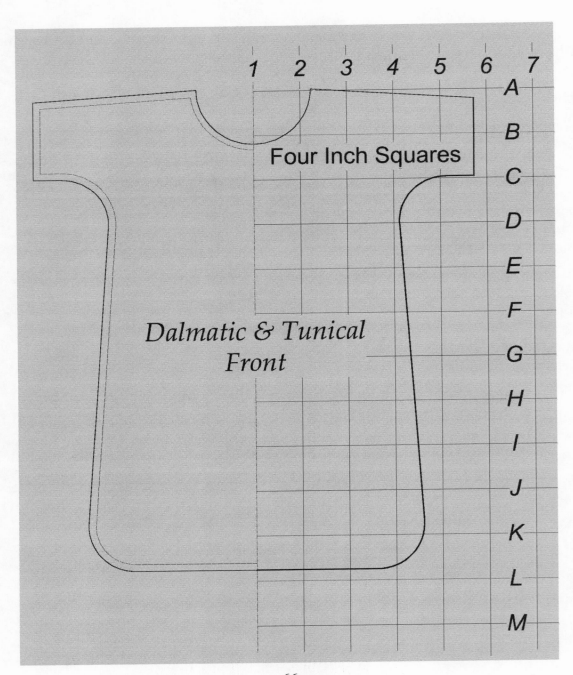

Four Inch Squares

Dalmatic & Tunical
Front

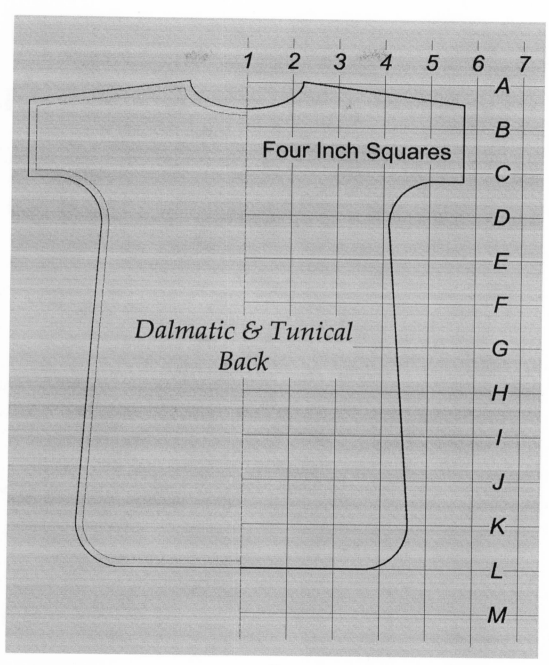

Four Inch Squares

*Dalmatic & Tunical*
*Back*

# Patterns for Stoles

Both traditional-looking tapered Stoles and longer straight ones are very much in vogue today. Below are patterns for both kinds.

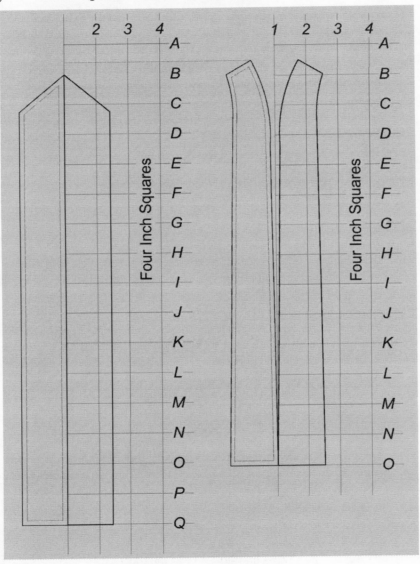

# Cope Pattern

Perhaps the most impressive of all church vestments is the Cope. Of course, it's completely superfluous in terms of usefulness. However, it adds a great deal in terms of dignity and as a symbol of authority.

In its origins, the Cope was a vast circle of cloth, with openings up the front and for the neck. The shape was essentially conical, and rose up high in the back. The pattern shown here is a much more modern one, with some shaping for the shoulders and hence more comfortable to wear.

The hood at the back of the Cope has undergone such a transformation that it is often nothing more than a flat, highly ornamented piece of flat fancy work. Two versions are offered below; one is of the flat sort and the other one a hood that at least looks like one.

Choose one according to taste as either one will do very nicely

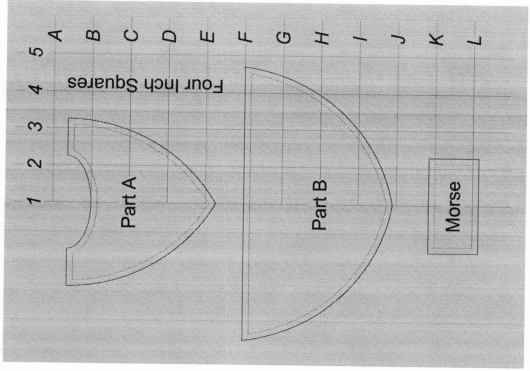

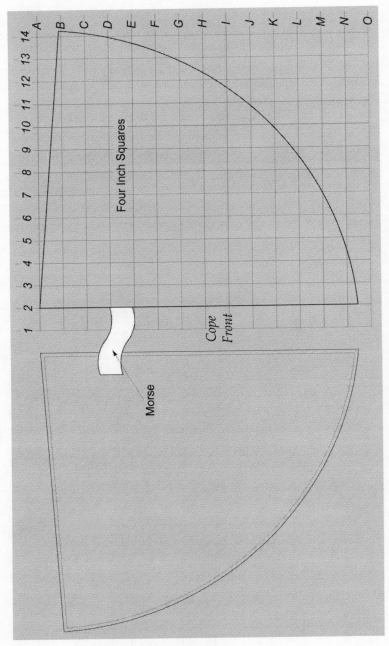

Four Inch Squares

Cope Front

Morse

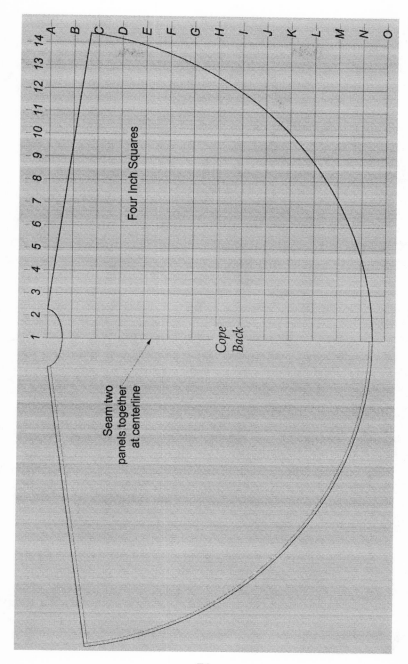

Four Inch Squares

Cope
Back

Seam two
panels together
at centerline

## Fabricating the "Silks"

The colored vestments above are generally referred to as "silks" no matter what fabric they have actually been made from. Silk was the usual fabric until the proliferation of the many man-made fibers that we can choose from today.

All of the silks are cut in the same basic way. The pattern is used for the face fabric, the interlining, and the lining.

**Chasuble.** Cut one of each piece from the front and back patterns. Cut the neckband pieces from the face goods only. First, apply trims to the face goods. Then, sew the front and back of the face goods together along the shoulder line. Assemble the lining and place it, face to face with the face goods. If interlining is used, assemble it and then place it behind the lining. Stack all three layers together in the proper order, Pin and sew them together all along the outer edge. This will leave only the neck opening open. Slash the steams, turn and press. Align the pieces of the neck opening and sew them together, raw edge out, ½" from the raw edge. Assemble the neckband as indicated on the pattern, so that there are four thicknesses, with the raw edges folded inside. Press. Unfold and stitch the outermost fold to the face of the garment, matching raw edge to raw edge. Refold the neckband, covering the raw edge of the neck opening, and finish on the inside by hand.

**Stole.** Cut one each of the left and right sides. Sew together at the top. The only customary trim is a cross, laid over this seam. Apply this cross and any other optional trims to the face goods. As with the Chasuble, stack all three layers together in the proper order, pin, and sew them together all along the outer edge, leaving the bottoms open. Slash the seam, turn and press. Turn the bottom raw edges inside the garment and sew closed by hand. Insert tassels or add fringe as desired.

Dalmatic and Tunical. The procedure is identical to the construction of the Chasuble. Use the Chasuble neckband pattern for these garments as well.

**Cope.** Cut the pieces for the hood that you have selected.

Flat Hood. Cut two pieces of face goods and one piece of interlining, using the "A" pattern. Apply trims to one piece of face goods. Stack all three layers together in the proper order pin, and sew them together all along the outer edge, leaving the top open. Slash seams, turn and press. Sew the top closed ½" from the raw edge. Set aside.

-or-

Open Hood. Cut one piece of face goods from the "A" pattern and one piece of interlining to match. Machine baste together ½" from the raw edge. This piece will lie against the back of the Cope. Cut one piece of face goods from the "B" pattern. Cut two pieces of lining, one from each pattern. Assemble face goods by seaming them together leaving the top open, Assemble the lining by seaming them together leaving the top open. Place lining face-to-face with face goods and seam, except for the interlined segment. Slash seams, turn and press. Sew open end closed ½" from raw edge. Set aside.

Cut one each of the left front, right front, and back. The back consists of two pieces of fabric seamed at the centerline. Cut identical pieces for the lining. Cut two pieces of stiffening interlining, 6 inches wide, to match the open side of the front pieces. Apply. Align the hood neck opening with the neck opening on the face goods, with the hood lying face up on the outside of the garment. Stitch in place 1/2" from the raw edges. Sew the left and right fronts to the back along the shoulder/side seam. Leave 5/8" on each side of the front opening unsewn for attachment of the lining. Either turn the hem up 5/8" twice, or apply seam binding and turn up once. Finish hem and press. Assemble the lining and press. Either turn up the hem 1" twice or apply seam binding and turn up once. Finish hem and press. Attach the lining to the Cope fronts, inserting the Morse in the left-hand seam. Press seam and turn. Turn the lining under at the neck opening and stitch in place.

## Surplice Pattern and Assembly

A Surplice is customarily made from a very lightweight white fabric. It is not lined and is very simple in its basic form.

The Surplice front and back are very much alike, and differ only in that the neck is cut somewhat higher in the back. The sleeves are huge, and attach to the body of the garment as shown in the pattern, thus making a raglan-type sleeve.

Cutting. Cut one back, one front, two sleeves, and two each of the front and back yokes.

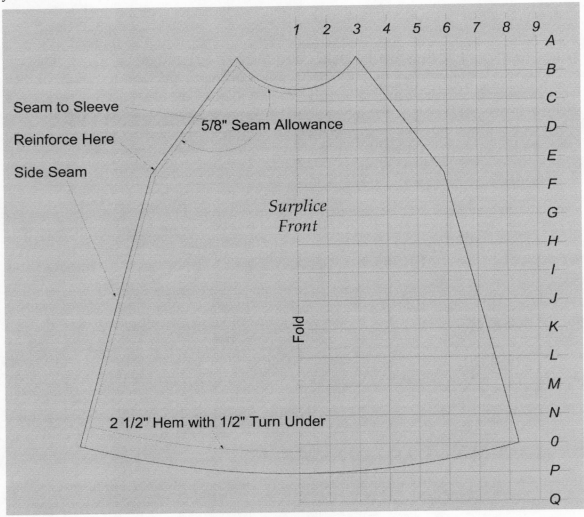

If you wish to make Surplices of different sizes, simply adjust the size of the squares on your paper to do so.

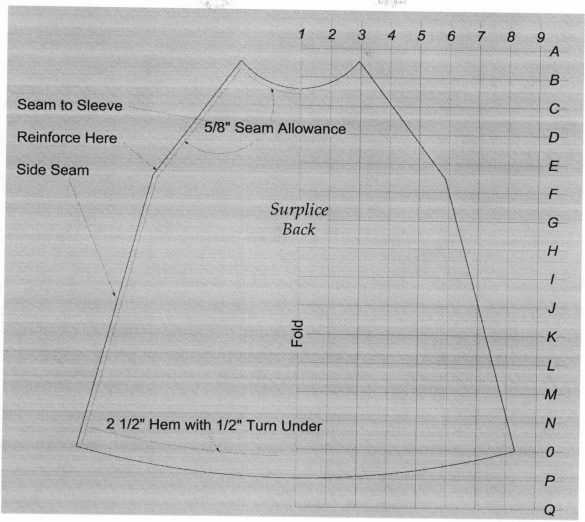

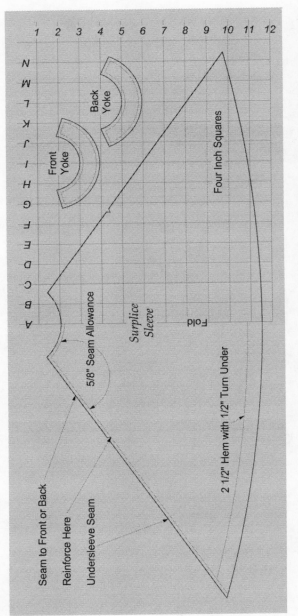

Assemble the two yokes by sewing the front and back pieces together. Then stitch the two yokes together along the side with the short curve, slash, turn and press. Turn up a 5/8" edge along the outer (longer) curved edges, baste and press.

Align the top centerline of the sleeves with the front-to-back seams to the yoke. Center the centerline of the front and back pieces with the centerline of the front and back yoke.

Then gather the sleeves and body of the garment evenly into the yoke.

Baste the garment in place, and then baste the yoke together front and back.

Finish the garment by stitching the three layers together, making a "sandwich" with the yokes as the bread and the body of the garment as the filling.

# Patterns for Stage and Screen

These patterns are not as authentic as the ones shown above, but are reasonable generic representations for stage and screen use.

## The Gown

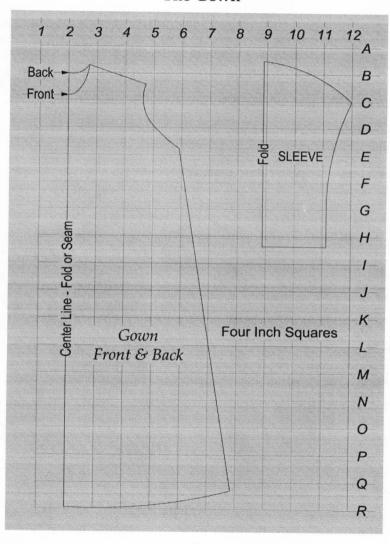

The basic pattern is shown. As can be seen, this garment is essentially T-shaped and the sleeve is gathered slightly, with more fullness in the upper back than elsewhere. In the alternative, the Gown can be cut with a more modern sleeve, but it should be as wide at the bottom hem. It will do nicely for any period. Face or bind the neck opening and hem the bottom and sleeves with a simple turn-up two inches to three inches wide. The front should include an opening at the neck about 12 inches long. It can be fastened shut with a hook and eye. The Scapular will cover this opening.

The waist should be tied with a cord (cincture) and a rosary may be suspended from the cord if desired.

## Monk's Chaperon

There are a lot of chaperon patterns, and almost any of them will do. A monks chaperon would vary from a layman's only in that it would have no lirepipe, and the bottom of the cape would not be daggled.

This is a simple two-piece pattern. Seam it along the edges that are not indicated as being open. Then hem or bind the open edges.

It can be worn over the head or folded back. The cape covers the top of the Scapular.

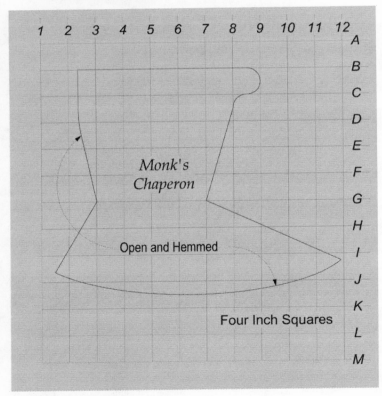

- 78 -

# The Scapular

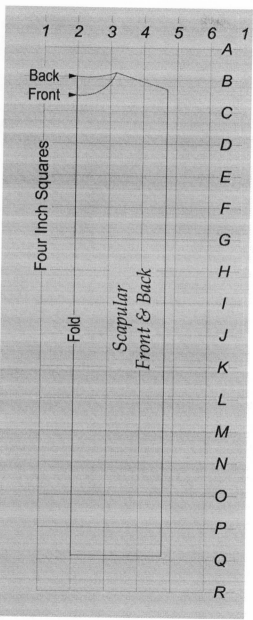

The basic pattern is shown here as well. As noted above, the neck is cut slightly higher and will cover the opening in the Gown.

The best way to fabricate this garment is to cut the front and back from face goods and a lining to match.

Seam the face goods together at the shoulders and then do the same with the lining.

Place the face goods and the lining face-to-face and seam along the long outside edge.

Turn and press.

Then turn up the bottom 5/8 inch and close. Slash the neck opening about ½ inch, turn in the neck by 5/8" and close.

The Scapular should be between 4 inches and 6 inches shorter than the Gown.

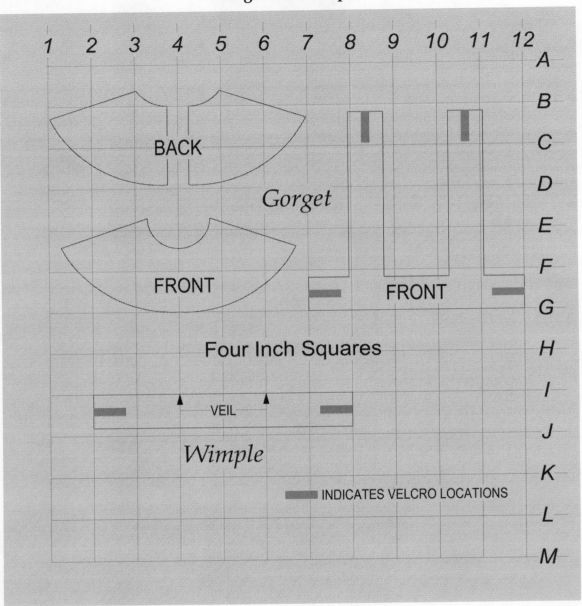

This is a fairly straightforward piece, made to fit just about anybody. It should be constructed from a fairly heavy and somewhat stiff white fabric. The front and back pieces may not require any additional stiffening, but the Front Upright and the Wimple probably will.

Seam the two Back Shoulder pieces to the Front Shoulder piece. Either line or hem depending upon preference. Cut two of the Front Upright pieces and seam together, leaving the top of the two uprights and the bottom open. Turn and press. Surge or otherwise close the two tops. Center the Front Upright on the Front Shoulder neck opening (face to face) and stitch around the neck opening as in attaching any collar. The ends of the collar will extend beyond the Back Shoulder pieces.

Next cut two Wimple pieces and sew them together along the long sides, turn, press and close the ends.

Cut a veil of thin, soft black fabric at least a yard square or longer if desired. Hem with a 1/4 inch hem all around. Center one side of the veil, back of veil to face of Wimple, and stitch in place 1/4 inch from the edge in the space indicated.

The wearer puts the Gorget on and fastens the back of the collar first. Second, the two uprights overlap on the top of the head and are fastened in place. Third, the Wimple is placed to encircle the head, just above the temples. Where the uprights and the Wimple overlap, additional attachment, preferable with Velcro, will be needed. (Nuns would have used straight pins with a white head.) The veil is then flipped back over the head and allowed to fall naturally. It is then pinned in place on either side of the face at the bottom of the upright.

It should be worn over the Scapular.

### Mitre

Begin the mitre by sizing it to the wearer's head. It is to be worn with the bottom parallel to the floor and fitting on the head just above the temples. The bottom line of the Base pattern should be 1/2 the circumference of the wearer's head plus 1.5 inches. Next, adjust the Outside Lining pattern to match.

From the Front & Back pattern, cut two each of face goods, lining, and medium weight buckram. Cut two pieces of face goods and two pieces of lining from the Lappet pattern. Cut one piece of lining from the Outside Lining pattern.

Apply trims to front and back pieces of face goods.

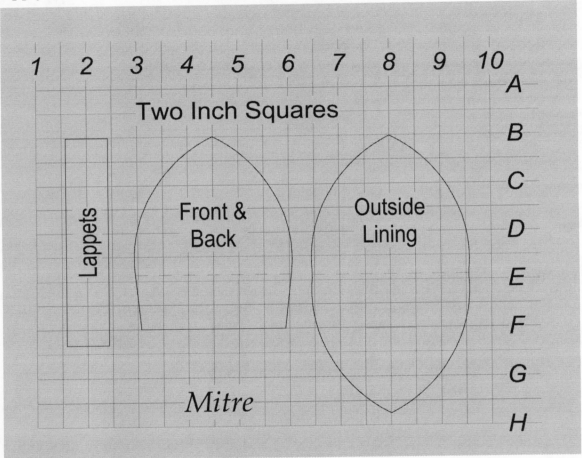

Assemble one side of the mitre in this order: (1) lbuckram to back of lining, (2) face of lining to back of face goods, (3) face goods, back to face of lining, (4) outside lining, face to front of face goods,

Beginning at the point at the top, sew a 5/8 inch seam along the curved side as far as the dashed matching line. Lock stitch and repeat on opposite side. Assemble and stitch the other side of the mitre in the same fashion.

Fold the Outside Lining along the dashed matching line. The two sides of the mitre should now be arranged with the Outside Lining between them.

Next, complete sewing each of the seams on the front and back pieces of the mitre, beginning at matching line and sewing down to the bottom edge. Be careful not to catch the Outside Lining with any stitching during this process.

Slash curved seams, then reverse both front and back pieces by pushing the pointed top towards the bottom of the mitre. Press.

Sew the front to the back of the mitre on the straight sides, between the dashed matching line and the bottom edge. This should be done by hand, using a strong thread and invisable stitching. The mitre should now be complete, except for a raw edge at the bottom. It should also fold flat. Align the top points and press thoroughly with the steam feature on high to re-stiffen the buckram.

Apply any trim, except fringe, to the face goods of each of the Lappets. Place the lining face-to-face with the face goods and sew along the long sides to make a tube. Turn and press. Turn up the bottom end of each lappet 5/8 of an inch and close by hand. Attach to of fringe 1/4 inch above the bottom seam.

Turn up the raw edge at the bottom of the mitre 5/8 inch and press. Then, measuring from the center line at the back of the mitre, place the lappets 1/2 inch on either side, with the raw edges aligned with the 5/8 inch turn-up at the bottom of the mitre.

Finish the mitre with a leather hatband, sewn in by hand 1/8 Inch above the bottom edge of the mitre.

## Needlework

There are many excellent resources that deal with ecclesiastical needlework. There is no need to repeat that excellent advice here. However, there are certain finishing techniques that can be used to advantage on even the most basic vestments. One of these is couching.

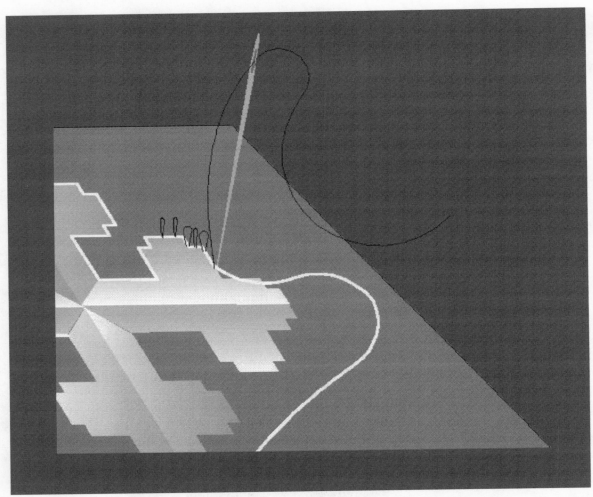

Once an appliqué has been attached to the face goods, it will be greatly enhanced if it is couched in place. This work consists of running a small cord or a twist of embroidery floss around the edge of the appliqué. It is fastened in place by small stitches that are the same color as the couching cord (shown here in black for the sake of clarity). The technique is a simple one: the needle comes up from the bottom just through the edge of the appliqué, over the couching cord and back down trough the fabric just outside the edge of the appliqué.

In the case of contrasting appliqués, couching cord of an analogous color may be used. However, if the appliqué is analogous to the face fabric, then a complimentary color should be applied to ensure that the shape of the appliqué stands out against its background.

A similar technique is often used to cover seams, but with a somewhat larger diameter cord, or with a length of galoon.

All of these possibilities provide a simple, if time-consuming way of adding a finishing touch and richness to the work.

# ENDNOTES

[i] *The Zeal of Thy House.* London: Victor Gollancz, 1949.

[ii] *Creed or Chaos.* Harcourt Brace and Company, 1949.

[iii] Genesis 3:6-7. New English Bible translation.

[iv] Mrs. Louie B. Meyer (Mr. Meyer was the Meyer of Metro-Goldwyn-Meyer later called MGM.)

[v] By which we mean *professional* in the sense of a position in society requiring a college education and often licensure as well.

[vi] Virillis, candida, praetexta, pulla, picta, trabea, purpura

[vii] The idea of a napkin or towel shows up later in the maniple; a short stole-like garment worn over the priest's left wrist at the Eucharist, and now obsolete.

[viii] St. Genesius is the patron saint of actors.

[ix] . Most modern tippets are made from heavy faille, although knitted black wool is still seen occasionally. Along with the surplice, the tippet is the proper attire for any minister, whether ordained or not, when conducting any of the choir offices. Simply put, the tippet is not a stole and therefore not properly reserved for the clergy alone.

[x] The bishop of the diocese carries the crozier with the crook facing forward. Assistant, suffrigan, and coadjutor bishops carry it with the crook facing them. Bishops outside of

their diocese do not carry one at all, unless acting for the bishop the diocese they are visiting.

[xi] Modern croziers come apart in two or three sections and are carried about in custom-made cases. No wonder the heathens mistake them for machine guns or grenade launchers.

[xii] The old name for Salisbury.

[xiii] A tippet is properly worn with these vestments, but is omitted in the illustration for the sake of clarity.

[xiv] During this contentious time, most of the clergy stayed at their posts and bishops in their dioceses. They switched back and forth between Prayer Book and Missal as the religion of the English monarch changed. Thus, more by accident than design, the Church of England's bishops remained in the apostolic succession.

[xv] The neck scarf eventually developed into the modern necktie.

[xvi] The underlying reason for the distinction is how one views the season of Advent itself. In the Roman church it is a "little Lent," whereas Anglican thought holds it to be a time of thoughtful anticipation. The color blue is in honor of St. Mary the Virgin.

[xvii] Not to be confused with purple, which is different color.

[xviii] Rose Brand is a supplier to the theatrical trade. Be careful to choose only fabrics marked IFR (inherently flame-retardant) or NFR (not flame-retardant). FR (flame-retardant) fabrics will have been treated with chemicals that stiffen them and are not necessarily good for the skin.

[xix] From the French *coucher*, meaning to lie down, lie low, or incline into place.

Made in the USA
Lexington, KY
04 September 2011